Grandma's Silver Series

Keeping A Promise!

by Diana Holt
illustrated by Josey Wawasniak

Order this book online at www.trafford.com
or email orders@trafford.com

Most Trafford titles are also available at major online book retailers.

Print information available on the last page.

ISBN: 978-1-4251-2007-8 (sc)

Our mission is to efficiently provide the world's finest, most comprehensive book publishing service, enabling every author to experience success. To find out how to publish your book, your way, and have it available worldwide, visit us online at www.trafford.com

Trafford rev. 03/06/2020

 www.trafford.com

North America & international
toll-free: 1 888 232 4444 (USA & Canada)
fax: 812 355 4082

I would like to dedicate this book firstly to my children,

Don, Randy and Tim

They have been with me through thick and thin, and have shared all phases and challenges with me. Thank you boys, I love you!!

Secondly, to all of my

Grandchildren and Great Grandchildren

who have given me more joy, fun and memorable moments in my life than they know. They have taught me to love, laugh hard and often, and to find delight in the simplest of things.

Thank You
to Josey Wawasniak
for the splendid illustrations.

A Special Thank You
to my many friends
for their endless continual encouragement.

Thank You to God
for being with me throughout my life, and never giving up on me. My work would never have been completed without God's help.

KEEPING A PROMISE

It was Grandma's day off work, so I called her on the telephone.

"Hi Grandma, I am lonely, may I come and visit you today?" Grandma said that she had things to do and had to take her telephone in for repair, because it doesn't work right. Grandma suggested that maybe another day would be better for me to go over for a visit.

"Grandma, I could come along and keep you company. I'll be super good."

"Well all right dear, because I know that when you make a promise, you always keep your promise. I can pick you up in half an hour, but you must ask mom or dad first. If it is ok with them, then I'll come and fetch you."

I went to check with Mommy. "Mommy, may I go out with Grandma today? I promise I will be 'Super Good'".

"All right dear, you usually do try to keep your promise", Mommy said.

I hurried and got ready and went outside to wait for Grandma. She was there before I came out.

"Hi Grandma, I'm ready", I shouted.

"Great, hop in 'Munchy'."

Grandma nicknamed me 'Munchy' when I was a tiny baby.

"Where are we going first?" I asked.

"Off we go to the Telephone Company, to see about having the telephone repaired or replaced", Grandma answered.

Off we drove to the Telephone Repair service man. It didn't take too long to arrive there. I followed along with Grandma, being very careful not to get lost. Mostly I held Grandma's hand.

At the repair service, Grandma lifted me onto the counter so that I could see the telephone man at work. First he looked at Grandma's telephone. Then he told Grandma, "I will exchange your phone for a new one". Grandma was happy, but she asked the man why. The repairman said, "the old one is worn out". Grandma happily said, "Thank you, Mr. Repairman".

"Come on Munchy, let's go and do some shopping".

"O.K. Grandma, I'm ready".

"Hold it a minute", said the repairman, holding a balloon. "I want to give this little fellow a balloon. This little boy was very good".

"Wow!" "Thank you! I will let my little sister play with it too. Thank you, telephone repairman"."My goodness, a good boy and a polite one too. I think I'll give you a handful of balloons for you and your sister".

I was so very happy. I blew up the balloons. Grandma bought some string to tie them too. I could hardly wait to get home to show my sister and share them with her.

"Grandma, I like to be a 'Super Good Boy'".

"Yes dear, people appreciate it when you are thoughtful while someone is trying to get something done. But, remember that you don't always get something when you are good".

"I know that Grandma. It just feels good when I keep my promise".

Printed in the United States
By Bookmasters